AF366390

LIVING FROM THE INSIDE OUT

A PHILOSOPHY OF LIFE
THAT WORKS

jeannette meier Ph.D.

LIVING FROM THE INSIDE OUT

A PHILOSOPHY OF LIFE THAT WORKS

jeannette meier Ph.D.

Índice

Living from the inside out by connecting to the heart is the gateway into the infinite Universe of love and creation that resides within you, encompassing your being and everyone else's into Oneness.

I purposefully use my experience to emphasize what it means to live from the inside out by showing you how I transformed from someone governed by the outside (people, surroundings, etc.) to a being connected to the heart.

I grew up being very shy until my twenties and very insecure for many more years because of what the outside world could tell of me.

I lived for others and not for myself.

In my thirties, I woke up.

Frankly, I did not search to awaken. I never had even considered this in my life. I did not know that I was asleep. But it happened to me one day when I decided to start loving myself, no matter what.

I felt alone, but always had a very close connection to my heart.

I knew deeply that the changes I had decided to make in my life were for the best. My heart expressed itself through my inner voice.

I bravely and faithfully followed this voice.

Connecting to the heart connects you to your inner voice, guiding you in your daily experiences to improve your decision-making and respond appropriately to every input that comes to you through your feelings, thoughts, and surroundings. This is what I learned through this awakening experience.

This book is part of "The Leadership Booklet."It contains poems I wrote after listening to my heart for advice.

These writings have accompanied me throughout my development into a socially-conscious leader. They are raw materials created from the heart.

These will serve you as they have served me to center myself into my Self, allowing me to be who I am and create what I love in freedom.

I have collected and arranged some of them into two sections: "Poems For You, Love" and a section that relates to these challenging times, and yet, a fantastic moment to grow the leader in you.

This book aims to empower and inspire you daily to live from the inside out.

You can read the poems in the listed order or randomly open a page to offer insight for the day.

Thank you from the deepest of my heart for accompanying me in love, uniqueness, and co-creation.

With lots of love and gratitude,
jeannette

Preface

By consciously connecting to the heart, your gateway to the Universe, you discover your Self and the Oneness you are.

Living from the inside out is defined by this conscious connection and by your constant observation, discernment, and response to your thoughts, emotions, beliefs, and patterns to affect your inside and outside worlds positively and continue growing into your Self.

I often wondered how to support someone in their awakening, for them to discover the love that they are, for them to uncover their limitless potential, or for them to know that everything and everyone is interconnected into Oneness.

My experience with the Positive iMPACT Movement and its community and the thesis and dissertation for the Doctorate of Philosophy have reinforced this exploration. They have allowed me to write The Leadership Booklet and this book while supporting my experience and showing you that anyone can connect to the heart, including yourself, leading you to a higher level of consciousness.

Connecting to the heart is a challenging task, especially when you have never experienced the unconditional love that you are and that surrounds you and when you do not know what it implies to create from the inside out, from your heart to the world.

It takes a willingness to continuously observe your thoughts, feelings, beliefs, and patterns to create from the inside out what you are: Love itself.

Everything in life takes practice, as does growing into living from the inside out.

Nothing is impossible; all is available for anyone if you take the time to explore, experience, and practice.

Once you have seen the connection to the heart, you will not want to return to the small and limited person you were, the one who sees life as only birthing and dying.

Observation is critical to integrate everything around and inside yourself to deepen your connection to the heart. You observe how your surroundings directly affect your thoughts, emotions, and actions and how these - your inner world - affect your surroundings.

This is a key element of living from the inside out, wholehearty by the mind serving the heart.

By doing so, your natural state is highlighted by moral values through loving, valuing, and respecting yourself.

Your view of the world changes into an optimistic worldview, opening your perception by discovering the infinite potential in you and everyone else. You will know that there is much more to learn and to grow into being who you are, from the heart into the world.

Some infinite books and practices support you in living from the inside out. Every author and every practitioner may highlight a different aspect of the power of the heart. Still, all agree in unison that you are unconditional love and Oneness when you experience the connection to the heart.

As there are infinite ways to connect to the heart, there's only one way that serves you: the one that you will discover yourself by listening to your heart.

Meditation is one of the practices that you can implement to explore and experience connecting to the heart. Journaling is another one. Anything can become your practice of living from the inside out if you stay present and observe who you are.

Reading serves to open my mind and to explore and integrate perceptions by feeling what to experience and practice next to continue growing into my Higher Self.

Nothing can be set as One-Size-Fits-All. Every person is different; everyone walks in their shoes.

I have been gifted with a mystical experience of experimenting unconditional love, but this is not what awakened me. It took me many years to realize my experience, even if I had never forgotten it.

I did not relate this experience to connecting to the heart until I started meditating and feeling this unconditional love and limitless existence within and through me, again and again.

Whatever you do, it is up to you to commit to continue practicing without expectations. Thinking of an outcome does kill the result itself because your mind is not serving your heart, and you are not letting yourself flow. Instead, your mind is taking control and not letting your Higher Self shine through.

It is my aim that this book leads you to explore, experience, and practice your way of living from the inside out, understanding the vast knowledge that you have within to freely choose your path, determining what best fits you through observation of your inside and outside worlds, holding relationships that affect you and which you affect, and comprehending the vastness of your existence by sensing the interconnectedness of everything through the loss of boundaries. You are me, and I am you. We are One.

I invite you to start living from the inside out to discover the love that you already are. There is no more extraordinary gift in life than knowing you are One with everyone and everything else.

Living From
The Inside Out

You Are One

I had a glimpse of the unconditional love that poured out of me when I decided to take action to love myself. This love provided me with the necessary and endless courage to start the adventure of knowing myself.

It took me many years to understand what it is to love and what it is to value yourself. One thing is to love yourself, and another is to value yourself.

They are interconnected, and when love happens, value happens. However, it takes time for value to be strong enough not to doubt yourself, even if love is already present.

Value came to me many years later through several experiences showing me how not valuing myself affected my being and doing.

As a teenager, I had the paranormal experience of living the unconditional love and Oneness. The limitless feelings with which I was embraced during this experience never left me.

This encounter gifted me with the precious knowledge of what Oneness means.

I will always be grateful for belonging to those who have experienced this phenomenon. It has left me knowing that we are not only a body.

I discovered my ability to fall easily into experiencing these incredible emotions by meditating, which only then did I associate with my prior out-of-the-body experience.

I did not consider that I had the intuitive knowledge to meditate, so I searched for this knowledge outside, in books and other people's methods. This led me to lose my way of meditating. I was still looking into the outside world to grow myself at that time.

Only when I consciously started to live from the inside out did I realize the importance of being who I truly am.

This is when I learned to love, value, and respect myself foremost, understanding that only through the love, value, and respect that I hold for myself can I love, value, and respect others equally.

Our state of mind merely defines the conditions we live in.

Our existence goes beyond our body, having the potential to create our outer world through the conscious identification and definition of our thoughts and feelings, our inner world.

Anyone can experience and practice this by willingly connecting to the heart without waiting for anything else to trigger it.

Through open-hearted conversations, meditation, and journaling, I have been exploring, experimenting, and practicing connecting to the heart, translating into words and actions the feelings that the heart emanates, responding to the world that I am creating through my thoughts, feelings, and attitude, and discovering what it means to live from the inside out. This is what I am sharing with you here.

In the next pages, you will journey with me into uncovering the unconditional love you are. You will understand what it is to live from the inside out.

Your mind and body are guided by your heart, creating your life from your conscious thoughts and feelings, interconnecting to everyone and everything through your being and doing, and experiencing the truth of your limitless potential.

The State Of Being

Love should be the state of being that prevails in everyone, or at least that which you should willingly explore, experience, and practice to be.

Because love is what unites you and me; Love melts everyone into the infinite universe that is part of who you are and who I am; Love highlights your values, perception, being, and connection to everyone and everything else.

We are One. We are limitless. You and I are in this together because we are creating our lives and co-creating this world by living from the inside out.

Love can change anything. This unconditional love is reinforced by connecting to the heart and the conscious observation and expression of your true being from it to the outside world.

You can discover the power of the heart through the experiences that life has gifted you with, that you intentionally and consciously explore and experience, and that you can practice to deepen your intuitive knowing and interconnectedness with others.

You will realize that you do not know anything. This is what will keep you inspired to keep growing into your Self.

"The only true wisdom is in knowing you know nothing.
By Socrates

You can consciously start unlearning beliefs and patterns that you have inherited or were inculcated to you by your teachers, parents, family, friends, community, etc. Your outside world has been shaped by a specific worldview set by your education and personal experiences, as highlighted by Jeremy Lent in his book *The Web of Meaning*.

Once you realize this, you can teach yourself to open up your perception, challenge yourself to look into other options to break your mind by reading about other possibilities, and respect any new point of view that is not yours.

The more you open your perception, the more you love, value, and respect yourself, everything, and everyone else, and the more you know that you do not know anything.

You are an endless bucket of lessons to learn, grow, and expand in this infinite Oneness. The mind exists to serve you through your heart-mind connection, not for you to serve it.

The power of the heart can be directly interpreted into the intuitive knowing and guidance from the Higher Self through the translation by the mind of the feelings that pour out of the heart, as explained by Nirmala in his book *Living from the Heart*.

In his book *Zen of Love*, Peter Cutler says that knowing can only flow through the heart through feelings. Journaling is an excellent example of this, which can be explored and practiced to reinforce the capacity to listen to the heart, to the Higher Self.

Living from the inside out connects to the vast and limitless universe of unconditional love that embraces you and connects you to everything and everyone. The energy of love expands beyond the being into the outside world, harmoniously impacting all other systems.

Everything is unconditional love that flows through you when connecting to the heart from the infinite universe that you are.

This true love unites everything, inside and outside of you. It dissolves your personality and melts everything into Oneness. It enhances your emotions, values, and perception by integrating you with all you are: Love itself.

A Journey Of Discovery

Explaining what awakening means is very difficult. It can only be understood once you have experienced it.

When asleep, you do not search to be awakened, especially not in the way you are experiencing it. You look for purpose, a life mission, but you do not know that your Why relates to becoming who you are.

Nevertheless, sometimes life spirals you to experience this awakening through what you are living, pushing you into survival mode.

When in survival mode, the heart is the one guiding you. This is the "One True Heart" that Peter Cutler mentions.

Once you have recognized your True Self, it is when you become your lover, and it is when you have awakened.

**" Love guides us from within the dream to wake up from the dream. In every experience of love, there is a taste of true enlightenment. Love is both the path to enlightenment, the bridge to enlightenment, and enlightenment itself.
By Peter Cutler**

Connecting to the heart encompasses living from the love for yourself and, from there, the love for everyone else. You become the one who loves you more than anyone else, and through it, you become the one who loves, values and respects yourself and everyone else.

Nothing is not feasible by you through the power of the heart. There is an inherent understanding that you are interconnected to a unified field of consciousness.

When you are love, you lose your persona. Undoubtedly, you maintain a particular aspect of your identity since you are human. Still, you have become borderless. Your values are enhanced through this inner knowledge that cannot be explained other than knowing.

Becoming Aware

Living from the inside out keeps you humble in who you are by staying in the present and enhancing your existence through a deeper awareness of your emotions, thoughts, and perceptions.

Who you are can be perceived more intensively when your awareness flows through your heart since the experience is much more noticeable when it comes from the heart than from the mind.

When you are aware of your thoughts, emotions, and actions, you know that you directly affect the outer world.

"Every thought you produce, anything you say, any action you do, it bears your signature.
By Thich Nhat Hanh

You are the creator of your life, the only responsible for what you are generating through who you are and what you do. Every thought, every word, and every action has an implication; this is an outcome outside and inside of you.

Anything you say affects others and yourself, firstly. Ultimately, you are the result of what you want to see. You cannot hide from yourself since you are the outcome of what you create and the first to experience this result.

"Things don't change until we change them. Or, rather, change ourselves.
By David Icke - *The Answer*

As you experience this for yourself, you also experience this for others. You know that you are interconnected and that anything you are and do affects others. You can feel it through your heart because it is your gateway into Oneness.

Becoming aware of who you truly are takes willingness, patience, and time. It requires the continuous observation of what happens inside and outside of you in every given moment and the understanding and correspondence post-adjustment of how you respond to every input from within (emotions, thoughts) or from outside of you (people, environment, etc.).

It is your responsibility to live from the inside out, getting to know who you truly are, disregarding those patterns and beliefs that do not fit you anymore, and understanding that you walk your shoes and not the shoes of somebody else. Hence, the time you take to learn and grow, and how you do that, belongs only to you. You are the one who knows what to take in (or not) and how it should serve you (or not).

One of the ways to learn to connect to the heart is through meditation. However, practicing meditation relies only on you. The way that you meditate is also merely dependent on you.

Meditation reinforces your possibility to awaken your heart to overcome the boundaries of your persona into what you truly are. It then supports you in observing your emotions and thoughts, which helps you deepen your values and open your perception of who you truly are.

When you become aware of your inner world, you change your life.

You have discovered your potential, the one that you recognize in everyone else, the one that has no boundaries, the one that is Oneness, the one that knows that change starts from within, from the inside out.

You know that unconditional love is you and that it encompasses everyone else. You are "pure awareness" or "pure consciousness" or "Universal Oneness." Different words define all but with the same meaning of boundless, powerful, and unconditional love you recognize through living from the inside out.

Poems For You, Love

Beautifully You

It is beautifully me who connects with you
Have you heard the birds singing?
Have you felt the light from the sun on your face?
Have you felt yourself in fusion with what surrounds you,
    being one and all with everything?

It is me who wants to enter your soul.
It is me who wants to awaken you from your long dream
It is me who wants you to look inside
It is me who wants you to be who you are.

Stay here within you
Look inside and feel my presence
i am here to awaken you
i am here to tell you how beautiful and powerful you are.

i was hoping you could allow me to show you a glimpse of
    what you are
Let me come in, and let me expand your being outward
This is me, who is You, a powerful being full of light and love
One with the Universe, One with all.

jem®

To Become One

i feel the expansion within me
i feel the love you are giving me
i feel the oneness with the universe
i feel the light that makes it all happen.

Expand beautiful soul to your outer world
Expand your being to what you came to do
Look inside and find your truth
Feel your gut and what it tells you
Follow your intuition, your most trustful wisdom.

Get into the light and become one with your Self
Show the Power of Being to yourself and who surrounds you
Become One with who you are and what you love to create
Expand and share your light
Love will cover you all over, for you will be One with all.

jem®

Freedom To Be You

Sometimes, you yearn for the freedom to live your life fully
You forget that it is you who has imprisoned yourself
It is you who has limited who you are and what you do.

You weave situations that complicate your existence
The simplicity of who you are remains intact
Your freedom is not lost: You have snatched it from yourself.

You do not want to see that being you is still a possibility
You believe that you will complicate your existence even
    more
By acting and changing what is bothering you.

The reality is that when you cross those mountains
Ahead of you and fully packed with complications
The valley of possibilities opens in front of you.

Life begins to gift you with opportunities,
You did not believe it possible
Existence becomes fun, fluid, and full of moments that make
    you vibrate.

You start doing what you feel
You share what you love
You live what you are.

With Freedom, you act according to your beliefs and values
You live happily with the rest of the world
You love what you are and what you create.

You are positively influencing those around you
You are at peace with your existence
You are in harmony with the actions you carry out.

You are capable of being free
Do not let fear block you
Your thoughts are those showing you the mountains of
    complications.

Take the first step
Realize that the mountain is only a tiny stone in your path
Look back and smile, and start living your life!

jem®

The Resilience In You

Many times, you do not know what you are passionate about
Sometimes, you work like a robot, fulfilling the hours
In the hope that the day ends soon to begin to live.

You have not had the opportunity to experience what vibrates
    you
You do not know who you are and what you love to create
You have yet to discover what limits you.

Some have been able to feel their essence, even for a glimpse
    of time
You acknowledge you want the same
Do not look at others; look inside of you!

Stay aware in the present
Every moment is a mirroring moment
Instants that have immense strength for you.

Those moments provide you with confidence
They give you the wisdom to know who you are
They awaken you to your passion
They lead you to what you want to achieve in life
They gradually move you toward your path.

There is no turning back when you identify your path
You know, it is part of you
You know that without it, you will get lost.

Moving towards your path is a difficult task
Build your confidence, learn to trust yourself
Encourage yourself to understand who you are and to value
    yourself.

One day, you wake up, and you know you can make it
You have the strength to fight against the wind and the tide
You are faithful to you, to your passion, and your life.

That driving force is infinite
It is pure resilience
It is who you are.

jem®

Walk In Togetherness

Walk your path every day, step by step
Do not lose your vision towards the horizon that brings you
    back to your trail
Believe and trust yourself
Meet people who vibrate just like you.

Walk together and grow
Believe in what you do and in what you are
Launch new challenges
Set your eyes on your steps and your horizon.

Live your passion
Share it with those around you
Create new ways for others to pursue their dreams
Be free and flow with who you are and with what you create.

jem®

You Change The World

From the power of your being, you change the world
From the Love that you are, you change the world
From the light that you are, you change the world

By changing your inner world, you change the world
By being who you already are, you change the world
By doing what you love, you change the world

Projecting everything you are from the inside to the outside
Being the Love that you already are
You change the world.

jem®

Share Yourself

Share your dreams, vision, and love
Be unique and expand your love of creating
Serve as inspiration for others to follow their heart
Show everyone's power and freedom
Being free to be and create what you love.

Your power of being is in expansion
Generating the positive impact you can only create
Getting together with others to unite and expand
For the common goal of living in love and freedom
Co-creating the New Earth.

No one else to guide you other than your heart and intuition
Powerful wisdom that lies within you
Not to be searched outside or in someone else
Believing in your power and in your freedom
To change this world through your existence.

jem®

Together We Are Limitless

Getting together with like-minded others
Through connection, inspiration, co-creation, and love.

Authentic and unique souls
Powerful beings with your dreams and projects
Vibrating through what you create.

Expansion through love by being respected
For whom you are
For creating what you love
For serving others through your being.

Empowering yourself through others
Feeling your spirit for what you do.

Aligning to your true Self
Learning through love and giving
All in the same cocktail of your existence.

Connecting with others without surrendering your Self
Enhancing your self-value and respect
Reinforcing your uniqueness by co-creating with others
Oneness and multiplicity for the New Earth.

jem®

Feelings

Feelings are a powerful connection to what you are
Feelings are translations of what you think
Feelings support you in realizing what you think.

Feelings can be changed
When changing your thoughts
The power is in you.

Stay alert
Observe your inside world
Feel the information that your mind is sharing with you.

You and only you can change your thoughts
Thoughts for a joyous life with yourself and for yourself
Creating your reality from what you are.

jem®

Be

Life can pass by so quickly
If you let it fly
Stay alert in the here and now.

In the here and now, everything is slower
You enjoy the moments and the surroundings
You observe and take in all the smells, sounds, and colors.

Living is being
Being is doing
It is existing by who you are.

Being is living from the inside out
Doing is creating from your heart
Through what you are today.

So, stop!
Feel the now
Breathe and be here and now.

Being here is the only thing that matters
The rest can wait; it will come anyhow, as it must come
Be, and let life bring you the most incredible gifts it has for
   you.

jem®

Just Be

We all are One
We all are love
We all are light
We are a piece of the Whole.

Let me be your guide
Let me be your friend.

Be what you are
i will guide you through it.

For that, you need to experience
For that, you need to feel
For that, you need to be open-hearted.

Because you already are
Because we already are
Just Be.

jem®

jeannette meier Ph.D.

i Love You

You and i are One
What i do, affects you.

i am sorry if I did not see this before
i just lived my life without care.

i now know that i affect you
The same way you affect me.

i want to honor you
i want to understand you.

i know i will never be able to walk your shoes
What i do know is that what i am and do, affects you

i Love you.

jem®

Everything Has Its Time

You want to be free to be who you are and to create what you love.

Your inner world and experiences will guide you to create through love.

You will stumble with your power of being.

You will not search for it.

You will become one with your dreams and vision.

The how will be unfolded as you walk your path.

What you see today won't be tomorrow.

The vision is short for what it is meant to be.

Stay connected to your Self to receive the answers when the time is correct.

It won't be before and not later.

All unfolds when it must unfold.

jem®

jeannette meier Ph.D.

Love Is All There Is

Love is immense
Love is all there is.

Share it with an open heart
Do not fear to get hurt
You are protected.

Nothing can hurt you
When you are being honest and free

Being who you are
Sharing who you are.

Love is always welcome
Love opens doors
We all are love.

Love forgives no matter what has happened
Love heals no matter how much you are hurt
Love is light
Love enlightens your path.

Love is You
Love is all there is.

jem®

Love Holds Everything

Expectations lead you nowhere
Love holds everything.

Just walk
And love will walk with you.

jem®

Honor Your Being

Sometimes, silence and loneliness are needed
To feel your spirit and what it tells you
For it is the one that guides you
To your path of becoming who you are.

No one else than you to love yourself
No one else than you to know yourself
No one else than you to become your Self
For you to walk in the path of your spirit.

Honor your Being
Now and in the past
Now and in the future
Now and Forever
For there is no time and no space in your spirit's existence.

jem®

All Is One

Listen to your spirit
Feel the love and joy
Stay connected with the light
Fly away to the infinite land of paradise.

Feel your immensity
Feel your limitless
Feel your expansion
Feel your infinite connection.

All is love and joy
All is bright and warm
All is infinite
All is One.

jem®

Deeply Grateful

You are flowing with the flow of the Universe
You are moving forward with your thoughts and actions
You are empowering yourself for what you are
You are feeling the abundance in you and around yourself
You are striving for what you believe and what you create
You are living for who you are today
You are deeply grateful for that.

Who you are today will change tomorrow
You are deeply grateful for that.

What you create today will change tomorrow
You are deeply grateful for that.

What you envision today will change tomorrow
You are deeply grateful for that.

You share the love the way you know
You inspire and empower others in the way you can
You awaken and evolve through your power of being
You embrace your spirit through your heart
You get together to co-create the New Earth
You are deeply grateful for that.

jem®

Meditation

Sitting, opening your heart
Your mind comes and goes
Your crown opens up
Little ants walking down your neck
The energy is flowing down your back.

Feeling the heat and the love
Feeling the unity and the intensity of the light.

Sitting and having time for yourself
It is time to get centered and feel your true Self
Through the power of being of who you are.

Feelings and treasure kept throughout the day
Present here and now for the day to remember.

jem®

jeannette meier Ph.D.

You Are Not Alone

We are many who believe in our dreams and vision
We are many who, through our change, create a better world
We are evolving spiritually by growing into our Selves
Many believe in who we are and what we love to create.

Working on what we love and expanding the positive impact
In a much more robust way, together with like-minded others
Growing impactful actions, spreading over the planet.

Together, we inspire and support each other
Enhancing uniqueness and purpose
Reinforcing who we are and what we love to create
And together, co-creating the New Earth.

jem®

Waiting For Inspiration

Waiting for the inspiration to come
Your creativity muse has left you for a while.

Maybe not today
Maybe just tomorrow.

Anyhow, here, and now you are
Working through your being for what you are called to create.

Love and respect for what is
Respect and love for what you do
No one else to love as much as you do
For what there is and will be forever

jem®

No Matter The Why

Feeling the energy flowing through you
Searching for a way to express what you feel.

You are changing
What you are today
It is not who you will be tomorrow.

Living by the now
Learning through the doing
Expanding through how
No matter the why.

Growing through your evolution
Trust and patience for what there is
Day by day, learning through the existence
Grateful for what you are and what there is.

jem®

Connecting Not To Forget

Waking up and sitting down
Waking up with the dreams on your lap
Waking up to awaken yourself.

Connecting to the source
Feeling its presence entering through the crown of your head.

The light that flows into your body
Feeling the connection, the heat, the energy
Feeling your heart vibrating, opening up
For it to remember who you are.

Being here and now
Feeling
Loving
Being one with all
Connecting not to forget the precious being that you are
For you to remember throughout the times of times.

jem®

Rebirthing

In the cocoon for a lifetime
Living encapsulated, not to be free
Being without being
Surrounded by fog with no perception of what there is.

Living with the world around you
Being without belonging
No connection to Mother Earth
Hanging in there to exist.

Birthing through awaking
In the beautiful spirit, you are
Falling protected into Mother Earth
To root yourself into the earth.

Energy flowing through you
Expanding your wings all the way out
Into this amazing world
For you to fly into who you are.

jem®

Kingdom Of Heaven

Walking to where you must go
Looking at the world with marvelous eyes.

Amazing nature that is so impressive
Kingdom of heaven all around you
For you to see and get connected
Teaching you to appreciate your fantastic life.

Kingdom of heaven that gifts you with everything
Kingdom of heaven for you to love
Kingdom of heaven for you to grow
Kingdom of heaven for you to create
Kingdom of heaven for you to be.

jem®

jeannette meier Ph.D.

Energy And Love

Energy flowing through you
Energy all around you.

Vibrating to enhance your vision
Vibrating to create through love
Vibrating to reach potential
Vibrating to expand into your whole.

Expansion for who you are
Expansion for what you create
Expansion through your freedom to be
Expansion for what there is.

All in One
One in All
Energy and love, here we are
For what you want us to be.

jem®

The Flow Of Life

Evolving to be who you are
Through awakening, you have become
What you are today and not tomorrow
Now and here, that is who you are.

Expectations are not to be lived today
Expectations are defined by your now
That is changing right now
To become what they are not.

Now defines how
By the choices you make now
Through what there is and who you are
Not to expect anything else.

Live by the day
Live by the now
Live by who you are
Live by what you love
For you to be guided through the flow of life
For whom you are and love to create.

jem®

jeannette meier Ph.D.

The Greatest Kingdom Of All

Love for who you are
Love for what you create
Love for what there is
Love for One and All.

No one else to love than yourself
Loving everyone and everything for your survival
Surrounded by the greatness of life
Independent of drama and kingdoms
For the existence of your limitless spirit.

Expansion and surrender
Loving and sharing
For your spirit to be
In the greatest kingdom of all: You.

jem®

No Matter What Happens

You are tackling your fears
You are creating what is in your path
Following your heart has not been clearer
For what you are through what you love to create.

You told yourself to jump off the cliff
No matter what happens, you are being yourself
No matter what happens, you are creating what you love
No matter what happens, you are living the best of the times
No matter what happens, you are safe in your power of being.

No better timing than the one that is
You are learning and growing along the way
Listening to your inner wisdom and remembering simplicity
    as the treasure to hold
For life to guide you, step by step into what is
Surrounded by love and light to co-create the New Earth
Through who you are and what you love to create.

jem®

jeannette meier Ph.D.

The Captain Of Your Ship

Today, you serve through your creation
That's what you are, and that's your creation
Tomorrow, you both will have evolved into something you
    cannot envision today.

You are not worried
You trust and love what you create
You do not know what will be
You are not supposed to know it, either.

Your life flows
You are not meant to stay stagnant in one place
Even the trees flow with the wind!

Today is not what tomorrow will be
Tomorrow is unknown, and this is beautifully perfect
Every moment is a surprise
Every moment is to be decided in action.

Becoming the river of the moments, this is you
Flowing in the now with what there is
Acting based on what you see here and now
Deciding based on your feelings and senses with your
    intuition as your compass.

Your creations will evolve
You will not know how and into what
This is not to be known
This is to be lived.

Allow yourself to flow, to act as you feel and as who you are

You are here to stay, to serve
You are here to sail with what the river of life brings you
You are here to create what has to be created
You are here to become what you already are
You are the captain of your ship.

jem®

Honesty, Humility, Respect

Honesty is based on truth
Honesty is the ability to respect yourself and others
Honesty is intertwined with humility and respect.

Taking the time to empower yourself
Value and respect yourself for who you are and what you
    create
Respect and admire everyone's individuality and uniqueness.

Limitless potential through who you are and what you love to
    create
Inspiring others through your open heart
Sharing your passion and enthusiasm, humility, and respect.

Respect for yourself, for what you think, and what you act
Integrity for who you are and for what you create
Positively impacting with honesty, humility, and respect.

jem®

Time Is Past. Now Is Time.

Trust in what is to come
Love what surrounds you
Conquer what you desire
For it is to come if it is done with love.

Disappear the illusion from you
It is the ego that creates the addiction
None is vital, and all is fake
Constructed by men with the desire to build their castles.

No matter what or who
It is up to you to dismantle the illusion
Your power of being from the center of the heart out to the
    world
Each of you, together, with who you are.

No time to be afraid anymore
Time is past. Now is time
Trust in who you are and in who you are to become.

No matter what they say or invent
Love will prevail through the hearts
Believing in who you are and what you do through the times
    of the times.

jem®

What Is To Come

When you feel like a blank page
When you know that your story is still to be written
When you know that life will unblock what has not surfaced
    yet
When information comes from everywhere and in different
    forms and colors
You observe.

Your feelings and intuition are your guides
No one else, just you.

Understanding what surrounds you
Letting your path evolve
Surrendering and learning
Through your experience and open heart.

Letting go of what you can
Learning to let go of what you cannot
Evolving through the support and mastership of who
    surrounds you
Loving along the way.

For what is and what is to come.

jem@

Trust

Be trustful to who you are
If others go one way, you keep believing in your way.

Trust in your intuition and gut
Even if you must go alone
Even if no one believes.

Follow your guide
Create your steps
And you will reach where it is for you to walk.

Trust in your self-lead
For you will arrive where your heart has taken you.

jem®

Staying Calm, Staying Here

You know you must stay calm
It is about staying here
No judgment. No time
Just here.

Being aware of what there is
Your state of mind and your thoughts
Aware of being aware
Being.

A difficult task
Here you are anyway
Being aware of your thoughts
Letting go for whatever must come when it has to come.

jem®

Positively Impact
The World

Express who you are
Human beings are powerful, so you are
You live in the freedom of your spirit
Love what you create and share who you are.

When you get to the center of your being
You acknowledge that you are amazingly powerful
You are then in sync with your Self
And no matter what, you respect yourself and everyone else.

Love yourself above anybody or anything else
Respect yourself and respect others for who they are
Share and love through your being
This is how you positively impact the world with who you are.

jem®

jeannette meier Ph.D.

Word And Light

Powerful lessons opening your vision
No casualties in life with no creation.

Creation through word and light
Word is love, and love is all
Light is you; you are light.

Divine creation of being
Magic and powerful being
Existing through inner wisdom.

You and no one else
Inside your heart and not outside
Thoughts and feelings by you
Word and light through you.

Divine and magical being, trust in you
For you to create your reality
You are. You create
Word and light forever.

jem®

These Are Times

These are times of knowing yourself
These are times of loving yourself
These are times of expansion
These are times of change.

Connect with yourself; love what you see
Find your essence; this is your authentic and unique you
Be who you are and expand yourself
From your inner world to the outer world.

Let go and stay light
You do not need anyone else than yourself
Be you and share yourself with who you want to be
In freedom, love, and respect for everybody involved.

Be the change you want to see
Start with yourself
These are times to be and create, now and here.
Nowhere else.

jem®

jeannette meier Ph.D.

Be What You Are

Be who you are
Be who you want to be
Act as if you are now, and you will be.

Let your being flourish from your heart
Deny your mind. Listen to the heart
Trust your inner voice that knows your truth.

Be and let go of what you know it is not from your heart
Feel the love, the calmness, the peace in you
The joy that your heart shares with you.

Enjoy this moment and the wisdom
Express what is
Just be what you are.

jem®

Let Yourself Be

Let yourself be free
Let yourself express who you are, what you are
Let yourself love and be love
Let yourself show love
Let yourself say love.

You are here and now
Do live your life
Let yourself be free to be.

All rely on you
For you are part of the Whole
Let yourself be.

jem®

Stay Loyal

Keep your eyes open
Stay here and now
Listen to your heart.

You will find your answers with an open heart
They will come to you through your intuition
You will feel the truth of what is true.

You know how to feel
You know when something is "right" or "wrong"
You know what it feels to know.

Stay loyal to your feelings
Stay loyal to your heart
Creativity is to be found in your heart and not in your mind.

Creativity comes from being
Being defines creation
Creation determines action.

Stay loyal to your heart
Stay loyal to your intuition
Stay loyal to your truth.

jem®

In The Now And Here

Be, just be here
Flow from the heart in the now.

Don't rely on expectations created by your mind
None will be the same as time will pass.

Everything changes
Moment by moment.

What you think now is good for tomorrow
Vanishes in the next moment.

Rely on your being
Choice by choice
Moment by moment
In the now and here.

jem®

Sustainability

Sustainability is not only financial sustainability
Sustainability includes well-being and evolution
Sustainability is part of who you are and what you create.

It is living well for many more years
It is being happy and remaining healthy
It is growing as a human with other human beings
It is growing your being and your creation.

You are unique with who you are and with what you create
Reinforcing your power of being
Positively impacting the world in sustainability.

jem®

Being And Creating

Sometimes, you feel as if you have fallen into a hole
In your process of being and creating
Not knowing where to continue.

Other times, you would have been nervous
Desperately tapping to discover where to step
Finally, moving forward to anywhere to surpass the moment.

You have been raised to fear that if you stand still
You will not reach success
Falling into desperation to do anything.

Today, you stand still
Today, you wait and trust
Today, you are patient until you feel the next step.

Your body speaks, listen
Your body tells you not to run anymore
Your body teaches you to listen to yourself.
Your intuition guides you where you have to move
You stroll, step by step until you can retake your average pace
Clearing your view and potentiating your being and your
    creation.

This is what shows you your way
This is what brings you success
It is creating through your being.

jem®

Detox

You are used to follow rules, steps, norms
Forgetting about your freedom to be.

You have come accustomed not to think
That you have an opportunity to do things differently
Do not give away your freedom
By following others blindly.

Express your uniqueness, always
There is no way you can be boxed into squares
Do not behave like a robot. Express your being
You are terrific as who you are.

Today, you give everything a second thought. Why?
You grew up validating if what you say or do is accepted. Why?

Why are you searching for approval outside when you are
your leader?

Start observing yourself when you search for approval
Check-in and approve yourself if you know it is right
Detox from the outside and nurture yourself with your inner
wisdom
No one is more knowledgeable about what is best for you
than yourself.

Skip the mind and follow your heart
Jump off the cliff and become who you are
Practice, practice, and practice flowing in freedom
Detox from the outside world.

jem®

Beautiful Dreams

My love, why can't you sleep?
What's waking you up?
Have you fallen into nightmares?

Sleep well, my love
For you to fall into beautiful dreams
Embraced in the love you have around.

No worries about taking it with you
Just love for what you are
For you to dream in peace.

My love, are you asleep?
What a beautiful dream you've fallen into
For you to rest for the day ahead.

jem®

Love And Universe

Let your thoughts navigate the day
Let your mind wonder around
Let her play her game
But don't play with her to forget about yourself.

She will always want you for her only
She's still young and pretentious
She's not able to see the grand picture
Of life that goes beyond the mind.

Listen to her, but don't follow her
Understand what she says, but disagree
Discern and focus on yourself
For you to grow outside your mind.

The universe is waiting for you
Don't limit yourself to your mind
Love goes beyond, and so do you
Since you are love and the universe itself.

jem®

Beautiful Spirit, Amazing Self

Beautiful Spirit, amazing Self
Thank you for your support
Thank you for your insights
For me to feel you through my heart.

Beautiful Spirit, amazing Self
Thank you for your guidance
Thank you for your love
For me to feel you beyond my heart.

Beautiful Spirit, amazing Self
Thank you for your advice
Thank you for your words
For me to connect with you every day.

jem®

jeannette meier Ph.D.

Jumping Into
The Unknown

Jumping into the unknown
Jumping into freedom
No more dictated by the mind
For you to flourish your being.

Decisions taken in the now
Decisions taken with the heart
No more jailed in by the mind
In freedom to experience life.

Actions created in love
Actions in response to the now
No more limitations by the mind
For you to return to who you are.

Freedom of action
Freedom of exploration
No more living in fear
For you to be who you are.

jem®

The Oneness Of Love

Your knowing cannot be expressed in words
It is for you to treasure and expand
No explanation is valid
No willingness is powerful enough
For you to awaken anybody else.

No right to change anybody's life
Respect beyond our existence
For you to trust that everybody has a moment in time
To be awaken from their dreams
For them to join you in your knowledge.

The mind encapsulates the thoughts
The thoughts limit the heart
Curiosity and observation become nonexistent
For anyone to open their perception
To join you in love and oneness.

You know that you can do none
Don't play with your ego cause you know you cannot do
What is for them to discover for themselves
By stepping out of the mind into the unknown
For them to fall into their hearts.

Be the change you want to see
Open perceptions through your heart
Let your ego vanish when asked
Why are you stepping outside your mind
For them to witness the beauty of love.

jeannette meier Ph.D.

Breathe deeply and go into your heart
Feel your knowing and potential
Extend your love to those around you
In compassion for what still must be experienced
In togetherness for the growth of oneness.

Don't fall into division
Don't let your mind play the game
Breathe deeply and listen with your heart
Embrace everybody with respect and trust
For everybody to feel the oneness of love.

jem®

When You Listen To Your Heart

Sit down and let yourself flow
Sit down and listen
To what others are talking
Through the openness of your heart.

Push your mind aside
Don't let it think it is there to talk
Today, your heart is the protagonist
From your feelings to your words.

Listen to your heart and flow
No matter what you're saying
Is your heart the one expressing
The knowledge of your soul that was hidden.

Keep your mind aside
Listen to your words
Discover the beauty of your talk
Through the emotions of your heart.

Sit down and practice
Experience the flow from the heart
The amazing potential you uncover
When you listen to your heart.

jem®

jeannette meier Ph.D.

Limitless Well

Love, what is it?
Not even close to what you have been told
Limitless Universe
That embraces you through yourself.

No love from the movies
No love from Valentine
True love that is in you
For you to expand through yourself.

Love for all there is
Love for everyone, no exception
Limitless well
For you to give and receive.

Your heart speaks to you
From the deepest of your soul
Beyond the physical and the emotional
For you to experience love.

Light within you
That calls you upon
To look inside and feel
The limitless well within you.

Check for yourself
Have the time and listen to your heart
See the light and the limitless Universe
That is in you and surrounds you.

Connection with all there is
Love for everything and everyone
Deep exploration and expansion
You are all, we are One.

jem®

Rediscovering Your Power Of Being

Feeling held by the love, there is
No matter the happenings around
Bonding with the Universe pulsating
Embracing humanity to expand
Limitless in their return
Into their Power of Being.

Many are still blind to the discovery
Of their potential to be
In freedom for who they are
In love for what they could create
Blind in their not wanting to see
The enormous beauty that surrounds them all.

No matter if you are blind or asleep
Everybody lives embraced in love
To open their eyes to discover
The light surrounding their being
Always and eternally existing
Awakening to be discovered and taken.

The Universe patiently always holding
Humanity to play and experience
To lose themselves in the games
To rediscover the love, they are
Through the freedom to be
For whom they are and what they create.

jem®

Contact Your Heart

Hang in there. Love is all you are
Contact your heart
Become One with yourself.

Let yourself pour out who you are
Never mind what anybody else wants and thinks
You are the owner of your life
Let your heart guide you through this ownership.

Become One with all of you
Become what you are in total awareness
Love yourself before anybody else
Listen to your heart. Listen to you.

Let all flow out for what is not in you
Check out your love for what you are
Feel the immense beauty of being yourself
Glowing from the heart to the world
Expanding in love for what there is.

No stronger power than this openness
For it guides you to your freedom
Freedom to be who you are
Freedom of sharing your power of being with the world.

jem®

jeannette meier Ph.D.

Listen To Love

Listen to the birds
Listen to nature
Love what it tells you
For you are part of it.

Fly like a bird
Sing like a wind
Dance like the trees
Limitless love for all there is.

Everything is connected
Including yourself
Feel your vibration
Melting with your surroundings.

All is connected
Everything is energy
Including yourself
Feeling your being one with all.

Nothing to fear
Nature is guiding you
Turn into love
For all to embrace you.

Love for what there is
Love for what there was
Love for what will be
Only now is true
Listen to Love.

jem®

Universality And Love

i am here with you, open-hearted
Let me come in
For love is the greatest thing you have.

Create with love, create with passion
All aligned to what is.

i will share with you what is
For you to spread the word.

Beware of who you come together with
Breathe deep and feel your heart
For it will tell you the truth.

Be grateful for what you are and what you learn
Nothing comes from nothing
All is based on love.

Listen to yourself and no one else
Listen carefully, be here and now
For what you are creating is based on universality and love.

jem®

jeannette meier Ph.D.

Deciding For Love

Your heart is pumping
Your mind is talking
Let the heart guide your mind
Not the mind guide your heart.

The heart sings its melody of love
The mind talks uninterrupted
For what are you going to listen?
Love or chatting?
Deciding for love is what expands your being.

You are love. We all are
Opening yourself as you are
Pure love energy, and joy
Positively impacting your life
Nurturing what surrounds you
A bubble of love and creation.

jem®

Your Heart Is Your Lover

Let your heart love
Let your heart be
Learn through your heart
To become who you are.

Listen to your heart
For what it has to tell you
Become its lover
Expand your dreams.

For you have come here
To awaken and live
From whom you are
To where you are.

No need to listen
No need to shout
Just being you with what you came
Wisdom all over you
From the inside out.

No need to cry
No need to follow
Just listen to yourself
Expanding your being
From the inside out.

Your heart is your lover
Your heart is your guru
No need to follow anyone
Just your integrity with who you are.

jeannette meier Ph.D.

Power of inner wisdom
Power of Love
Being in union
With you and all.

One with the heart
One with the world
In unity and trust
Living and expanding from who you are.

jem®

Thank You

Gifts of life
In love for life
In love for everyone
In gratefulness for what there is.

Listening to the heart
Thriving as guided
Embracing what is coming
Loving what there is.

Beautiful life; thank you for your teachings
Thank you for the love
Everyday surrounded
In the beauty of existence.

jem®

The Knowledge
That Is Within You

Opening your mind through your heart
For you to attend to your feelings
Sensations that guide your thoughts
Into the archives of the Universe.

The knowledge that thrives through you
For you to identify through your sensations
Understanding through your heart
For you to acknowledge in your mind.

Listen to your wisdom
The knowledge that is within you
For you to hold your truth
In integrity for who you are.

jem®

Any Advice For Today?

Beloved heart, any advice for today?
Breath and hold your hand on your heart
Feel the vibration in your body
Tingling from the heart to the crown and the toes
Information is getting through via sensations.

Transformations of feelings into thoughts
Thoughts that result from the sensations
Translations into words of wisdom
For you to write one by one
To then read in surprise and gratitude.

The beauty of the words that guide you
Throughout the day, in honor
Toward your guidance
Through the wisdom of your heart
Expressed in love and kindness
Through your body and mind.

jem®

Every Day Is Love Day

Today is a beautiful day of love, as every day
Having the possibility to give and receive
Through your being and doing
From the heart to the world.

Love through who you are
Love through what you give
Love through what you receive
Open-hearted through giving and receiving.

No need to have a special day to be love
Every day is love-day
Every day is for you to grow your leadership
Daring to be who you are and to create what you love.

Loving and valuing yourself
Loving and valuing others
Everyone walking in their shoes
In love and respect for yourself and everyone else.

jem®

In Presence...

The power of being that is you
This limitless potential that is you
Through your heart and being
Unconditional love that is freedom.

Love, Freedom, Peace
Incredible connecting energy of being
Everything being one and the same
Oneness in uniqueness and love.

Energy that is you and me
Borderless, limitless life for everyone
Connection no matter where
Together in time in the moment of being here and now.

Presence, love, freedom
Connection through the being
Intention and feelings that are borderless
In presence to create what you love.

jem®

Be Your Guru

Be your guru
By being who you are
Open yourself to your greatness
Be the love that you are!

Love is you
Love is everyone
Love is unconditional
Love is everyone and everything!

Project yourself outward
Allow yourself to be who you already are
No borders that limit you
Experience this limitless energy!

Be your guru
By being in service to yourself
By being in service to something greater than you
Because you are limitless!

jem®

The Love Of Self

Let yourself flow
To discover the Love of Self
Tap into that energy
Inspiring everyone else to do the same.

Once you discover this love
You uncover your limitless potential
And know that everyone
Has limitless potential.

The new way of being human
It is to be in love with yourself
And loving everyone else
Through your freedom to be.

There is no exclusion
There is love and respect
For everyone to grow their way
Through your growing in love.

jem®

Love Is Everything

Love is not the new marketing jargon you and i hear from
   politicians, corporations, and people who only want to
   grab the attention.

Love comes through your heart and not your mind
Love is not ego-centered
Love is all-mighty, encompassing you, everyone, and
   everything
Love is unconditional; no ifs or shoulds relate to it.
Love cannot be given or taken away
Love is you and i, and everyone, and everything
Love cannot be created
Love exists.

Be who you already are: Love!

jem®

Talk From The Heart

Allow yourself to be
Allow yourself to flow
Allow yourself to share
Be vulnerable!

Listen to your heart
Let your heart speak to you
Talk from your heart
Flow through your being!

Don't let fear overtake you
Don't let your mind block you
Don't let yourself fall into the trap
You have a limitless potential!

Change yourself to change the world
What you do, impacts around you
Be who you already are
An amazingly perfectly imperfect being!

jem®

Everyone To Become One

Everyone is love
Everyone is Oneness
No one above the other
For everyone is growing in this plane.

Awakening into your being
It is just the first step
In the path of discovering the Self
For everyone to thrive in Oneness.

The ego shows its power
For you to know it's just an illusion
Love is everything, and everyone
For you to discover you are nothing.

Nothing is everything
Nothing is love
No one more than the other
For everyone is the same.

No need to show off
When knowing you don't know anything
Nothing is all
For you to become everything.

Slowly but surely
Experiences show you the way
Integrating the love that you are
For everyone to become One.

jem®

Step By Step, Now By Now

You walk step by step, Now by Now
Living free, safe, and in love for every moment
Whatever comes will come
As you walk, be here
Look inside, follow yourself
That's how you build a marvelous future
In freedom and love
And in respect for yourself and for everyone else.

jem®

jeannette meier Ph.D.

Love Is All There Is

Love is all there is
No cliché, and no advertisement here
Unconditional love in you
Because that is who you are.

Why do you not see it?
You are caught in the outside world
That banalizes and diverts everything
For you to stay lost in superficiality.

Why cannot you feel it?
Love is not only in relationships
Love is you, and me, and everyone
For you to grow into who you are.

i might sound crazy to you
But give it a try, and be love in everything you do
You will discover your limitless potential
That which you already are.

jem®

The Universe Is In You

The Universe is in you
You are the creator of your world
That which surrounds you
And that which is in you.

Listen to your heart
The door into the Universe
The one that is unconditional Love
And that which is you.

Open the door
Let the Universe enter your life
Limitless potential on your doorstep
And that which you are.

jem®

Honor Yourself

Your body, your temple
Nothing else holds you safer
For you to grow into your Self.

Your mind, your connection
That which integrates you with your consciousness
For you to grow into your Self.

Your heart, your guru
The one that guides you into Oneness
For you to grow into your Self.

Honor your body, mind, and heart
These are your soul mates
For you to grow into your Self.

Nothing else accompanies you in life
Than yourself through that which you are
Honor the universe in you
Since you already are love, consciousness, and Self.

jem®

Shall Love Guide You

Shall love guide you
To know that Love is the answer
To all the darkness in this world
To dissipate through the light that you are.

Shall love guide you
To know who you are
To acknowledge your limitless potential
To enlighten your existence.

No need to fight
No need to argue
No need for war
Just be the love that you are.

Shall Love guide you
To discover the Truth
To be who you truly are
To co-create the new Earth.

jem®

Let The World Unfold

Let the heart guide you
In love for who you are
Let the world turn
In love for what you create.

There is no turning back
There is only advancement
For there is nothing to fight for
The truth shall be revealed.

Ask yourself the question:
Where am i in all this?
Let your heart answer you
Are you living in the Now?

Do not fight what is not for you
Love instead through who you are
This is you being you
Not following what you are not.

Let the world unfold
Everything has its purpose
Today, you do not see
Tomorrow, the new Earth is here.

jem®

My Love, Hang In There

My Love, hang in there
This is just you pushing yourself
For you have come to be who you are
The veils must fall to uncover your truth.

My Love, hang in there
This is just a moment in your life
For you to grow and discover what there is
Unconditional love in all there is.

My Love, hang in there
This is just you wanting to be
For you to discover your limitless potential
Dissolving drama to be who you are.

My Love, hang in there
This is just the last drop of the illusion
For you to be in freedom to be
Thriving through who you are in Oneness.

jem®

Remember Who You Are

Love, enjoy the day
Give whenever you can
Receive with an open heart
For you to grow your power of being.

Smile, lighten up your day
Share with an open heart
Listen with all your presence
For you to shine your light.

Love, raise your vibration
Hug with all your heart
Embrace with all your love
For you to feel your power of being.

Give, expand your universe
Kiss with everything that you are
Receive with all your heart
For you to return to your soul.

Remember who you are
You are love
You are peace
You are limitless.

jem®

Your Nature

Trust the universe
Trust the light
Live your life in the Now
For your heart to guide you.

Insights flowing through you
Insights for you to respond
Live being guided by your heart
For you to fulfill your nature.

Nature of being who you are
Nature of creating what you love
Live with an open heart
For you to co-create the new Earth.

jem®

jeannette meier Ph.D.

You Are Divine
In The Here And Now

The sacredness is with you all the time
No need to search for it
Because you carry it within
For you are Divine in the here and now.

Live from your heart
From the love that you are
Let it guide you through all times
For you are Divine in the here and now.

Move your mind away and focus on your heart
Let your mind translate your feelings
Let it be in service to your heart
For you are Divine in the here and now.

Feel what your heart is telling you
Stay present with its energy
Expand your being through your heart
For you are Divine in the here and now.

Connect with others through your heart
Be in relationship with who you are
Stand in Oneness with all you are
For you are Divine in the here and now.

jem®

The Portal To Your Self

Your mind is not in control
It is your heart that serves you
By being the portal to your Self
For you to expand in this world.

Your mind is just a servant
That has believed to be the King
Making it difficult to give up
For it to be the servant of your heart.

The heart is the portal to your Self
The one that is who you are
The one telling you that you are limitless
For you to be in freedom in this world.

To be in freedom is to be who you are
The mind in fear is losing control
It plays with you for you not to see
The limitless potential you carry within.

The portal to your Self is open
You are the one creating the world
You are the one in control of your mind
For it to finally be the servant of your heart.

Do not let this opportunity escape
It is your responsibility to let your Self shine through
Your mind to take a step back
For you to flow in freedom to be.

jem®

In These Challenging Times...

In these times, when society is pushing you to follow others; when you are trying to figure out what is happening in this world; when the moon, the sun, and the planets are playing their game for you to reinforce or reinvent yourself...

I emphasize the superpower you already have by being who you are because our future (yours and mine) relies on us being free to express our uniqueness and co-create from there.

In today's world, we are being pushed to depend on the outside world rather than our insights and discernible capacity.

Division and fear are the energies shared for people to forget about themselves and blindly follow the narrative.

The division is not only used to separate you from others. It is used to separate you from who you are.

As you do not know yourself or do not love or value yourself enough to stay in integrity for who you are, you can be easily controlled by fear.

Everyone is the same and, simultaneously, different, authentically unique but equal in beliefs, values, and willingness to positively transform this world in integrity with who you are and what you create.

I worked in the United Nations and lived in NYC when 9/11 happened. I followed MSM until December 2001, when I discovered how I was being manipulated to live in fear.

However, still conditioned by the UN, I continued believing in certain things, such as the Sustainable Development Goals (Agenda 2030), which I used for my social enterprise.

Luckily, in parallel, I continued with my responsibility to know myself, growing spiritually.

This provided me with the insights to understand that here, too, I was being manipulated and that control is occurring in almost every aspect of society.

Today, I do not watch any TV, nor read or listen to MSM, and I have left Facebook, Instagram, and WhatsApp.

Today, I am free to select and discern the information I consume.

Today, I do not believe in everything that I am being told: I listen, I investigate, I feel, I discern.

Today, I have learned to love, respect, and value myself, forcing me to continue being who I am: Love, uniqueness, and co-creation.

I invite you to do the same.

You are love, uniqueness, and co-creation. Remember it.

In These Times

In these Times
i am grateful for having met you
For having you walking with me
This path of growth and return to the spirit.

In these Times
i am delighted to have you in my life
For learning through your uniqueness
This amazing, perfectly imperfect being that you are.

In these Times
i let myself be guided by my heart
For you to learn through me
This guru that i am for myself.

In these Times
i recognize your power of being
For you to thrive with me
In the co-creation of the new Earth.

In these Times
i am in love with you, with myself, and with everyone else
For Oneness to grow in everyone's heart
This unconditional love that is everywhere.

In these Times
i gift you with your love
For you already are who you are
This reflection of yours that is mine.

jeannette meier Ph.D.

In these Times
i remind you of your limitless potential
For you are in freedom to be
This leader in you walking with me.

jem®

126

i Am, What About You?

i am a Socially-Conscious Leader
i am being who i am and creating what i love.

i serve, i want to be of value to others
No one is asking this to me.

It is my responsibility and my own choice
i live with integrity and dignity for who i am.

i am in freedom
i own my life.

i am a courageous warrior who fights for my wins
i have come to experience expansion and commit to my
    growth and purpose.

What about you?

jem®

My Clowns

i have always been a creative child
No boundaries to what i envisioned to create
Always knowing that creation needs commitment
i seldom quit before finishing what i was creating.

Today, i continue to envision
i do not quit, but i go step by step
Pausing, when necessary, to know the next step through my
    heart
Observing my path as it unfolds before my eyes
To slowly but surely create what i see
In the way it is meant to be, no less, no more.

You find clowns everywhere in your life
Pushing and pressuring you to take specific steps
To fall into the pitfall that is not meant for you
But for many to follow by not seeing what they are meant to
    see.

My clowns are here with me
It might be the clowns i sometimes have in my head
Never mind what they tell me
My heart is my guidance
And my power of being is my freedom.

jem®

Today, It Is About You

You, who is the leader of the future.

You, who are crazy enough to commit to your growth

You, who is in integrity for who you are no matter what

You, who lives from the inside-out, knowing that you might go against the current, but you don't care

You, who are connecting with like-minded others, to get supported for the changes you bring into society

You, who sometimes feels alone but who courageously continues your quest because you know that's what you came to do

You, who believe in co-creation and not in competition

Yes, it is about you!

jem®

"
Here's to the crazy ones.
The misfits. The rebels.
The troublemakers. The round
pegs in the square holes. The ones
who see things differently.
They're not fond of rules.
And they have no respect for the
status quo. You can quote them,
disagree with them, glorify, or
vilify them. About the only thing
you can't do is ignore them.
Because they change things.
They push humans forward.
And while some may see them
as the crazy ones, we see genius.
Because the people who are crazy
enough to think they can change
the world, are the ones who do.
By Rob Siltanen

You Are Free!

Are you entrapped?
Don't you see it's you!
You are limitless
A fantastic expression of your spirit!

Where are your bars?
Why did you build them around you?
You are free!
A beautiful expression of who you are.

Free yourself of your prison
Free yourself of what you have built
Don't be afraid of expressing who you are
Don't be scared to be you
Let your beauty flow to the outside
Let your being become you.

Don't be afraid of others
Every thought comes from your mind
None will be the way you think
You won't know until you don't try!

Look back into what lies behind
See yourself now into what is
Expand yourself to the outside
For an amazing explosion of freedom
Freedom to be who you are and create what you love!

jem®

The Leader That You Are

Today, more than ever, you are living in unprecedented times.

The world continues turning as events continue unfolding....
But there is light in all darkness!

You are preparing yourself to become brighter to outshine
    whatever must be lightened up by your example of being
    and doing.

No matter what happens in your outside world, when you
    continue to center on your inside.

Your power of being cannot be taken away by anybody or
    anything.

You are the author of your life; you are your lover, your judge,
    your guru... !!!

jem®

Wake Up

Wake up, open your eyes
Crack your mind open
Still asleep?
Take control of yourself!
Only some things you have been told are true.

Read and investigate anything that doesn't follow your
    patterns
You will discover how your mind controls you
To think from where you always have been standing
Let it say: "Are you crazy?"
But give it a thought
That is not everything you know that you know.

You know what you have been taught
But is this true?
The truth is that you don't know
Because you have not lived it
So open your eyes
Doubt on everything, think twice
Discover how everything affects you.

Tell the truth to yourself: nothing and everything is true or is
    false
Because the reality is that you don't know
You only know what you experience
Only from there, you can share
With humbleness and respect
About your experience and truth.

jem®

Be Who You Are
And Create What You Love

The world needs more people like you.

Prepare yourself to become brighter to outshine whatever must be lightened up by your example of being and doing.

You have come here to expand, experience, and commit to your growth and purpose.

You live in integrity and in dignity for who you are.

You are a mighty human being who respects and values yourself.

Let your new self flourish by becoming a courageous warrior who fights for your wins!

jem®

Follow Your Majesty

Today's society is being divided by the puppeteers who
    everybody follows
Why do you need to follow someone?
Why do you need to idolize anyone?
Where are you growing to?
When your potential is so high for you to be your guru!

Don't you see that everybody else is like you?
A human being with existential issues like you
Someone following someone else....
So, who do you follow?
Have you thought about that?

Why don't you follow yourself?
You are the majesty of your kingdom
You always will be
You are responsible for your life
You always will be
You choose in every moment what you think, say, and do.
Isn't that amazing?

Why are you giving away your power?
Look inside of you. Take a moment. Pause.
Who do you see in the mirror?
Who's smiling at you?
Who's griming at you?
Who's behind that face?

jeannette meier Ph.D.

The majesty that you are in your own temple/body
Become aware of your being
Become aware of your thoughts
Love yourself because you are your guru
Look inside and discover who you are!

Let Your Majesty shine and for you to bow in Your presence
There's no one greater than you in this world
Follow yourself, and society will unite
Connect and co-create through your uniqueness with respect
    and dignity for who you are and everybody else.

No one else to follow other than you:
Your guru, majesty, your highness, your president, YOU.

jem®

In Freedom To Be

This is me, writing from who i am
A beautiful being like you, who is in power and freedom to be
who i am.

Fear controls society.
Fear is nothing more than a possible outcome created in your
mind.

Reality will always be different than that which you are
expecting
Your mind and perceptions are based on your current
moment in time that is not your tomorrow
How do you know what's happening next?

You will only know something once you experience it.
Isn't this marvelous?
This is the beauty and the freedom of existence
None is real
None is what you think it will be
So why live in fear for something that doesn't exist?

Follow your heart!
It is your answer and your guide
When it knows, you know
The rest comes from your mind, nurtured by your
surroundings
Don't let this be the source of your being!

Dare to be who you are and let everything else fall aside
Nurture your being through your heart
Who knows better than yourself?
Those who live their lives and walk their shoes?
How could they know more about you than yourself?

Get together with people like you, who respect and love you
    for who you are
Be in freedom to express the fantastic and powerful being
    that you are
You have a purpose.
No matter what it is, it is uniquely yours!
Will you give it away?
No! You have come here to experience, learn, and expand.
Let yourself shine and lighten up this world for the benefit of
    all!

jem®

The Shore Of Oneness

Lost in the sea of society
Thriving to ride the wave of love
Getting immersed in the beauty of existence
Gliding toward unity and love.

Riding the waves together
Balancing ourselves in integrity
Letting the wave of love guide us
Toward the shore of Oneness.

jem®

jeannette meier Ph.D.

Be You In This World That Needs You

You are dissolving the boundaries
You are breaking through the darkness
You are giving birth to a new world
The world for you to thrive and expand
To be who you are in freedom and safety.

No more fear, no more lies
No more fake numbers and news
No more puppeteers with puppets
The world is showing you everything
For you to choose and decide to live in truth.

Truth for what there was
Truth for what there is
Truth for what there will be
The world that permits you to choose in freedom
For you to experience and expand with who you are.

This world is in you
Don't wait for others to tell you this
Live in freedom to be who you are
Expand in safety for what you create
Shine throughout darkness with your light.

Light outshines darkness
Light expands infinitely
Light enlightens others
Just be you in this world that needs you
For you to shine your light.

No need to do more
No need to fight
No need to fear what there is not
Just be you in this world, knowing what there is
For you to outshine through who you are.

jem®

jeannette meier Ph.D.

The Potential Of Connecting To The Heart

Let the storm rise outside you
Keep calm and in peace inside you
Don't let the world steer you up
That is what is wanted
For you to react to the outside.

Let the world continue
Let the acts flow their scripts
Let the actors do their work
Do not join the play
For it is not you to die for them.

Stay in your center
You will be pushed left and right
It is up to you to stay where you are
In your responsibility for your Self
In safety for your freedom to be.

Don't play the game that is not yours
Stay resilient to your truth
Respect others with their acts
It is not you standing on their feet
Let them experience their truth.

The world continues turning
Stay connected to your heart
Light up for others to calm with you
No words and no play are needed
For you to transform what is around you.

Don't play the game
For it requires to follow the exact instructions
It is not meant for you to fall into the pit
Even if everybody is playing
Stay in your center for everybody to discover
The potential of connecting to the heart.

jem®

jeannette meier Ph.D.

In Love For Who You Are

Theatre unfolding around you
Actors playing their scripts
Everything moving behind the curtains
The spectator becomes a player
Unaware of the role that they are playing.

The piece is already written
The milestones already set
The players do not know the play
As spectators integrated with the script
Sleepwalking in their lives.

Watchers awake
Constantly observing
Living from the inside out
Continuously discerning
Living in truth for who they are.

Awakening others
With respect for who everybody is
Everybody has the right
When choosing free will
To sleepwalk in their lives.

Observation of what there is
Free will to choose
There is no need to play in a script
When aligned with your truth
And in love for who you are.

jem®

Evolving In The Freedom To Be

What is observation?
What is love?
Nothing other than your life.

What is fear?
What is drama?
Nothing else than your experience.

You don't want to grow through fear
You don't want to evolve through drama
Then, focus on discovering the beauty of life
By observing and loving no matter what.

Fear and drama will disappear
Your mind will be freed
Your spirit guides you in the unknown
For you to continue evolving in the freedom to be.

jem®

jeannette meier Ph.D.

Let The River Flow

Don't rush
Let the changes sink in
Accept that none can be controlled
Let the water flow.

Don't jump in
Let everyone be
In freedom and love
For the flow to stream.

Don't control
Let it find its path
With the potential it brings along
For everyone to thrive.

jem®

This Is My Vision

i share with you my feelings and vision
By daring to be who I am and to create what i love
A world co-created in love and togetherness
Through uniqueness and co-creation.

Nothing else than being love by being who you already are
Exploring, experiencing, and practicing being
Positively impacting through your being and doing
In co-creation with others like you.

Giving and receiving through your heart
The one that guides you into living from the inside out
Sharing who you are through the one that you already are
In love, respect, and togetherness for a better world.

jem®

Today

Today, You do not know what there will be
But every moment is a present
To construct the future that will be
All is accepted since it belongs to your growth
And the expansion of your being.

Today, you dare to be who you are
In freedom and love
No matter the outside world
For you to live from the heart.

The more you experience living inside out
The more you witness the positive impact
That ripples through your heart
Into the outside world you live.

A leader is to be who you already are
Living from your heart to the world
In harmony with everyone else
And co-creating a better world
Through your doing, in love, and togetherness.

jem®

Awakening To Your Purpose

Being who you already are is
Understanding how true you are to yourself
Without straggling in the day-to-day
Flowing like a stream in your life.

Being who you already are is
Connecting to your heart
Listening to your inner wisdom
Being guided into the freedom to be.

Being who you already are is
Flowing into the simplicity and easiness of life
Feeling your path as you take the steps
Flowing to become the best of yourself for yourself.

Being who you already are is
Checking in with the energy of Self
Exploring the love that you are
Positively impacting through your being.

Being who you already are is
Being open to what comes to you
Letting everything happen to grow
Flowing into your freedom to be who you already are.

jem®

Be Who You Are

Being who you are is being
In freedom to be who you already are
In truth to yourself
For you to flow in love and togetherness.

Finding your true self
Through your energy and not through your mind
Listening to your inner voice, the one that is your Higher Self
Speaking to you for you to listen and be guided in love.

Flow in your life through your heart
Allowing yourself to flow without the mind-controlling you
Feel your feelings by checking in with your energy of Self
Explore, experience, and practice connecting to the heart.

Be open to things that come to you
Do not search or run after anything or anyone else
Stay present in your heart to flow in your life
Just be and flow in love and togetherness.

jem®

Discovering Who You Are

When you discover your power of being
You love, value, and respect yourself
It doesn't matter what happens,
When you are who you truly are.

The world is changing from the inside out
Being who you are for yourself and no one else
You are the example of the change you want to see
Inspiring others through who you are.

Discovering who you truly are by connecting to the heart
From the inside out and not from the outside in
What beats your heart? What makes you feel alive?
Start your journey of discovery to find your Self.

It is your responsibility, with love and respect
To every day explore, experience and practice to be
Flowing through the heart, freeing yourself to be
Changing the world from the inside out!

jem®

Building Your Path

You are the relationship you have with yourself and with the
    world
You are your perceptions, your thoughts, your actions
You are the example you want to see in the world
You are the sole one who walks your shoes
Don't wait for others to do the walking for you
Since it will never be what you require to grow into your Self.

Belief in yourself before in anyone else
Be your lover in respect for yourself and for everyone else
Be responsible and have integrity for who you are
Be your guru because no one else will guide you better than
    yourself
Don't wait for others to do the walking for you
Since you are building your path with who you already are
    today.

jem®

A Glimpse Into Freedom

Being who you are is liberating
Being who you are is inspiring
Being who you are is empowering.

You grow through uniqueness and co-creation
Anywhere and at any time
By daring to be who you are
Living from the inside out
Discovering your limitless potential.

jem®

It's About Perception

Perception, what a beautiful acknowledgment
Everything depends on where you are looking at it
No one will ever know how to walk your shoes
Everyone will always see it from their shoes.

Open your view when listening
Respect the sharing from some others' shoes
Know that you always see it from your shoes
No one is right, and no one is wrong.

Everyone is walking in their shoes
Never forget that those aren't yours
Listen and respect their point of view
Let everyone walk their path in respect and love.

jem®

Today, You Walk Your Path Naked

Looking back on what you have been
Observing who you are today
You realize the path that you walked and that which you have
   created.

Today, you can strip yourself of everything
Staying naked with that which you are
In freedom, love, and integrity for who you are.

Today, you can tell the world that everything you have
   created
It has been to grow into your Self.

It is that which you are today
That which your persona carries with it
In value and respect for who you are
In union with everything and everybody else.

You do not know when you have grown
Other than realizing that you do not know anything
And what you know depends on the path you have walked.

Today, every step you take is in love, uniqueness, and co-
   creation.

Today, you walk your path naked
Only wearing the "I AM".

jem®

jeannette meier Ph.D.

A Socially-Conscious World

What a beautiful vision
That of a socially-conscious world
No one has angst in life
Everyone is living from the inside out!

There are no sacrifices. Everyone thrives through themselves
Being supported via the giving and receiving
A true community of love, value, and respect
Everyone has what they need through their uniqueness.

Learning and growing through the heart
Living from the heart to the world
Flowing in togetherness and Oneness
Allowing everyone to be in freedom.

Flowing through relationships
Giving and receiving in the moment in time
Living from the heart without must's and should's
Through equal uniqueness and perfect imperfection!

No one is better than the other
Everyone being their leader
Everyone being the example that they want to see
A world without governments as of today.

A world full of love, respect, and values
Freedom, dignity, and power of being in and for everyone
Uniqueness defines what you love to create
There is no need to limit your limitless potential!

jem®

May You Awaken
From The Land of Dreams

May the light shine over you
May love awaken you
From sleeping in the dreams of life
For you to discover Truth.

May you become light
May you be embraced by love
Awakening to your amazing Self
For you to be who you already are.

The light that you shine
The love that you are
The freedom that you have always been
For you to awaken from the land of dreams.

jem®

jeannette meier Ph.D.

Growing Into The "i AM"

Let yourself flow
Into who you are today
For you to grow into your being
While discovering your limitless potential.

Let yourself be who you are
Today, and every day
For you to uncover your potential
While growing your uniqueness.

Let yourself be in freedom
In integrity for who you are
For you to become love
That which you already are.

Let yourself be love
Loving and valuing everyone else
For you to unite in freedom
Into the Oneness of everything and everyone.

Let yourself co-create
Through love and uniqueness
For you to grow into your Self
And together thrive into Oneness.

Leave your creations behind
Those that have grown you into the "i AM"
For you to expand into Oneness
And together, co-create the New Earth.

jem®

i See You Rebels

i see you, rebels, socially-conscious leaders
i see your power of being
i do not associate it with today's world
i associate it with your heart.

Yesterday, today, and tomorrow, you are who you are
It is you who changes the world
Not by fighting, but by being in integrity for who you are
In love for yourself and for everyone else.

Today, someone might call you other names
Yesterday, it was you, and it was all ok
Someone who did see the world with your eyes
A clairvoyant following your heart.

Today, you continue being who you are
In uniqueness and in Oneness
Expressing the love that you are
For everyone to acknowledge their limitless potential.

Always a rebel by heart
Always being the change you want to see
In freedom for who you are and for everyone else
Being love, uniqueness, and the leader in you!

jem®

**"The Rebel has no enemy.
He simply has a vision that the
old is finished.
By OSHO**

No Fear, No Walls

No fear, no walls
In love for yourself and everyone
Uncovering your limitless potential
For you to know your truth.

No fear, no walls
In trust for what there is
Walking your path in freedom
For you to potentiate your uniqueness.

No fear, no walls
In freedom to be who you are
Discovering your power of being
For you to return to your Self.

No fear, no walls
Openness and interconnectedness
Love and Oneness
For everyone to unite in togetherness.

Unconditional love
Unites everyone from within
No fear, no walls to create
When in Oneness through who you are.

jem®

Thank You

Thank you for the new day
For me to grow with you
Thank you for the experiences
That have shown me
Everyone has their path.

Thank you for the love
For me to never feel alone
Thank you for the extremes
That have allowed me to discover
The power of unconditional love.

Thank you for the company
For me to evolve with everyone
Thank you for the relationships
That have reflected to me
The lesson to learn to grow.

Thank you for the path i walk
For me to share the love that i am
Thank you to everyone i know
Who have and are walking their path
For everyone to grow into their Selves.

Thank you for the love
For me to grow in uniqueness
Thank you for the growth
That we all are experiencing
To reinforce co-creation.

Thanks to everyone
For being who you are
In love, uniqueness, and co-creation
In awareness to your power of being
We together co-create the new Earth.

jem®

jeannette meier Ph.D.

Today, More Than Ever

Today, more than ever
You are responsible for who you are
Feel your body
Listen to your thoughts
Be the change you want to see.

No more excuses
You are your guru
Listen to your heart
Observe your mind
Be the change you want to see.

Follow your wisdom
You are limitless potential
Observe your feelings
Listen to your inner voice
Be the change you want to see.

Be you:
The one who is responsible for your Self
The one who is your guru
The one who is limitless potential
The one who can change the world
By living from the inside out.

jem®

In Responsibility For Your Self

You are your body
You are your mind
Listen to your heart
For the wisdom in you to protect your spirit.

Your spirit whispers to you
To protect your body and mind
In responsibility for who you are
For you to grow into your Self.

No matter what is told to you
No matter what you hear
Turn inside out
For you to listen to your heart.

Your heart is wise
Your mind recognizes your heart
Return to your spirit
For you to fulfill your purpose.

Your purpose is to be who you are
Nothing else to search for
In integrity for who you are
For you to thrive into the wonders of life.

You are your guru
The one responsible for your Self
In love and respect
For you to protect your spirit.

jem®

jeannette meier Ph.D.

What Does It Matter

What does it matter
The currency you're told to use
When the value is given by yourself
To anything you choose to use to trade?

Do you remember salt?
It's on your table today
Before, it was used for trading
The people gave its value.

The people define society
Not the other way around
The individuals create the change
By living from the inside out.

Today, a digital currency is pushed in
Who tells you what to use?
The old money being devaluated
For you to fear you're losing it all.

Freedom cannot be taken away
When not in fear of what others tell you
When in your Power of Being
Knowing everything, it's just a stage.

You give the value of anything
No matter if it's zero in the mind of some
When you trade with others like you
You give the value.

It's a matter of perception
Open your eyes to your inside
For you to know that the power is in you
And not the other way around.

You give the value
It's your choice to be in freedom
That which you were birthed into
And no one can take it away from you.

jem®

jeannette meier Ph.D.

i Have Been Missing You

i have been missing you
In this field of emptiness
No individuals standing
For their freedom to be.

Society is just a concept
Created by the sum of individuals
Where are you in all this?
i have not seen your being.

i have only seen society
Raising for individuals
But who governs you?
Isn't it you for yourself?

Society is just the sum of individuals
Why does society have a saying?
When you are your own master
In this life to grow yourself.

Yesterday, society might have been useful
Today, laws have become obsolete
Today, you are your authority
Through your freedom to be.

No one is better than yourself
In love, respect, and value for who you are
Knowing everyone else is you
Love and Oneness in all you are.

Wake up, my friend
You know what's best for you
You are the individual to be
For you to choose in freedom and love.

Love goes beyond the matter
Society is just a concept
For you to stay in prison
Avoiding being the leader in you.

The responsibility is yours
It has always been
To live in freedom and love
For you to grow into your Self.

Individuals with limitless potential
Love and Oneness in everything and everyone
Communities co-created through freedom
For everyone to thrive in the new Earth.

jem®

jeannette meier Ph.D.

The New Earth That Is Already Here

In freedom and connection
We thrive in co-creation
This new Earth is about you and me
Through freedom, love, and uniqueness.

Freedom is being who you are
Living from the inside out
For you to love and value yourself
Being the guru that you already are.

Do not let anyone push you
Not governments, not nations
You are in freedom to be
In integrity for who you are.

Love is the force that drives you
To expand into everything and everyone
Discovering that you are not alone
For everyone connects through and with you.

Change starts from within
Do not search it outside
You are the one to follow
For yourself to thrive in uniqueness.

Uniqueness defines your path
In love and co-creation
Let your authenticity shine through
For everyone to learn through you.

Who you are is your purpose
The enlightenment of your spirit
For everyone to see you shining
Inspiring the world around you.

Co-creation through love and uniqueness
In freedom to be who you are
Everyone being their guru
Flowing and growing in togetherness.

Freedom, love, and uniqueness
A blend of who you already are
In respect and integrity for everyone
Co-creating the new Earth that is already here.

jem®

jeannette meier Ph.D.

The Path Of Socially-Conscious Leadership

What this earth needs
Is you and me in freedom
To follow your heart
For you to return to your spirit.

In this playground
You have come to discover
The power of being in you
For you to co-create the new Earth.

No need to follow others
No need to disrespect your being
The wisdom is solely in you
For you to grow the leader in you.

The illusion of love
The ego playing around
The collective being manipulated
For you to uncover your individuality.

The uniqueness that is in you
Grows stronger every day
Discovering your limitless potential
For you to know you and i are the same.

The Oneness that you are
Through the love that you are
Knowing that you do not know
For humility to grow in you.

The path of socially-conscious leadership
Is only one step away
Everyone being the leader
For love to thrive on this earth.

No need for governments
No one above the other
You are your leader
For you to co-create the new Earth.

Love, uniqueness, and co-creation
Natural law for all mankind
Value and respect in integrity
For everyone to thrive in Oneness.

jem®

jeannette meier Ph.D.

The New Earth

What is the new Earth?
A utopia from illusion
Or the co-creation from the heart
For everyone to be in freedom?

Freedom to connect to the heart
Freedom to be who you are
Freedom to create what you love
For everyone to grow individually.

Growing into your Self
Is nothing else than being unique
Living from love being love
For everyone to thrive on this earth.

Love, value, and respect
Are the values leading the earth
Created by you and everyone else
For everyone to lead the new Earth.

Leading through love and uniqueness
No laws to be created
When knowing not to harm anyone
For everyone to live in freedom.

Co-creation is born through this power of being
Freedom for yourself and everyone
Love and uniqueness co-creating the new Earth
For everyone to grow into the Self.

The new Earth is not a utopia
The new Earth is co-created by you
Here and now, through your change
For everyone to enjoy the love that they are.

jem®

Do Not Play In
The Game Of Fear

Focus on what you want to create
By being who you are
Recognize what is happening around
But do not play in the game of fear.

Listen, see, observe, and know what is happening
Clown world all around you
Focus on your being
On that limitless being that you already are.

The ego plays with you when being in your mind
Allow yourself to be aware of it
Let go of those thoughts
And focus on what you love to create.

Inspiration comes through your open heart
Thrive for yourself to be your leader
Everything else comes along
Allow yourself to be pulled back into your energy.

It's natural to be there once in a while
It's about being the human that you are
Respect and understanding for yourself and everyone
Supporting through love for everyone to thrive.

Celebrating love and awareness
Not playing the game when you are pushed into
Different points of view come upon you
Open your eyes and heart for your leader to join.

Focus on your uniqueness and co-creation
Do not strengthen what you do not like
Re-focus on the awareness of who you are
Shift back into your limitless potential.

Perfectly imperfectly selves
Holding each other together
Co-creating a new Earth through the being
In freedom, love, uniqueness, and celebration.

jem®

jeannette meier Ph.D.

Believing In Your Limitless Potential

Would love to co-create the new Earth
Believing in you and myself
In this limitless potential that we have
As anyone on this beautiful earth.

Learning to observe and be
Unlearning patterns and beliefs
For you to grow into who you already are
In freedom and in love to be.

Flowing in your being in the now
Releasing the control of your mind
Letting anything unfold
Through the love that you already are.

Nothing can go wrong
As you already know through your Self
Creating in the now
Through the limitless potential that you are.

Co-creating the new Earth with me
Through your courage and uniqueness of being
Loving the leader that you already are
In responsibility, taking action for yourself.

Inspiring me through your action
Courageously showing your uniqueness
Elevating human consciousness
Through your limitless potential.

jem®

The New Day

Today is a new day
Tomorrow is a new day
Every day is a new day
For you to be thankful for another day.

The new day may be a new year
It may be Christmas, Easter, or another day
What you define it to be is
For you to be grateful for another day.

You die every night and resurrect every day
What an amazing opportunity to expand
Into the being that you already are
For you to grow in uniqueness, love, and co-creation!

jem®

Listening To Your Wisdom

Being pushed into doing things
Does not bring anything with it
Only stress and mind control
For you to disconnect with who you are.

Resting into your being
Resonates with who you are
Following your heart
For you to grow into your Self.

Listening to your inner wisdom
No to that which others tell you
Discovering the power in you
For you to acknowledge the guru in you.

Disconnecting from the chatter
Uncovers more about who you are
Observing through your heart
For you to grow the Leader in you.

No one to follow other than yourself
For you to live in humility and Love
Growing your amazing Uniqueness
For you to co-create the New Earth.

jem®

You Are Your Leader

You have been guided to think in a certain way
By not letting your Self shine through you
In this prison of doing and of not growing
For you to follow someone else other than you.

Your mind is used to follow others
Especially the ones that are "authority"
Don't you see that they are your public servants
For them to service you through what you pay?

You have been told that they are your leaders
The leaders that you are to obey
But they are your public servants
For the leader that you are for yourself.

No need to follow anyone
When not aligned with who you are
The leader in you guides you in love
For you to grow your uniqueness in freedom and respect.

What is wrong or right you already know
This has been in you since you were born
Love, value, and respect for yourself and everyone
For you to co-create the new Earth.

You are your leader
You respect and love everyone's guru
Explore, experience, and practice being love
For you and everyone to thrive in togetherness.

jem®

jeannette meier Ph.D.

You Are Your Purpose

Where is my purpose?
Have not seen it around for a while
Maybe it is just me being who i am
No matter what i do or where i am.

Unlearning to live in this world
Through living from the heart
That which i was born with
And forgot by living from outside in.

Beautiful spirit, you are still with me
Never left me, even if i had forgotten you
Today, growing into who i am
By listening to the heart.

Observing this clown-world
Everything is as clear as the blue sky
But hidden through the vails of desire
That is what i have been taught to see.

Opening my perception
It has been my sole responsibility
For me to grow into my spirit
To discover the wonders of life.

Living from the inside out
Doing miracles to unveil the truth
Observing manipulation and greed
For everyone to return to their spirit.

Love is all you are
Nothing else is needed
For you to be your guru
In integrity for who you are.

The new Earth is waiting for you
Through the wonders of your heart
Nothing else than your purpose to be who you are
In love and togetherness, co-creating the new Earth.

jem®

jeannette meier Ph.D.

The Worlds Are Colliding

The worlds are colliding
One, showing openly what is happening
Another, pushing for what is to come
Where are you on this earth?

The worlds are an illusion
For you to awaken into who you are
Not playing along in the games
In these clown worlds that are not for you.

The worlds are a mirror
For you to discover your truth
Looking beyond this theatre
For you to know the leader in you.

The worlds are disappearing
As you discover your Self
living from the inside out
In integrity for who you are.

Not playing the game anymore
In love, dignity, and togetherness
Letting yourself flow through the heart
In this new Earth, that is you.

jem®

You Are Freedom And Love

You are love
An expression of all there is
Nothing else than love
In Oneness with everything and everyone.

So why do you separate yourself?
Your mind is playing you tricks
Letting the outside world control you
When you are almighty and sovereign.

Look inward into who you are
Recognize your limitless potential
Ditch the limitless perception
That you are just a tiny human in this world.

There is nothing more away from the truth
The Universe is in you
You are freedom and love
For you to create your existence.

Forget about what you have been told
Open your heart and your eyes
Expand your perception into all there is
For you to co-create the new Earth.

jem®

Break Free

i am who i am
A divine being like you
Experiencing the world
Though what i am: Love.

i have come here to grow
i have come here to be in relationship with you
i have come here to be love
All the rest is an illusion.

Spirituality is not love and peace
It is to be who you are
It is to be love
It is to express your divinity here and now.

The world is fake
It is what you came to break free
Open your heart to who you are
Expand beyond your five senses.

Everyone can do it
You and i are limited beings
The Universe is in us
For us to escape the illusion.

jem®

The AI Mold Is Being Broken

How do you know your Truth?
The heart is here to tell you
It is the one that is guiding you
For your heart is the door to your universe.

The illusion shows you synchronicities
The mind collects these as true
The heart guides you via feelings and sensations
It is the one from which you know the truth.

Intuition is the door to your Higher Self
Intuition comes from within
It does not show you messages outside of you
For you are Divine from the inside out.

When you know, you know
This is what comes through you
No need for messages from the outside
For your Truth is within you.

Today, we see a glimpse of reality
AI is capable more than what we see
Do not underestimate the illusion you live in
For it has been ruling for thousands of years.

Today, the veils are falling
Truth is coming through stronger
Knowing that it comes from within
For you are limitless through your heart.

jeannette meier Ph.D.

Lies cannot be hidden anymore
The game and the players are shown
In the hearts of many on this Earth
For love and unity prevail.

Your paths are unveiling
Through the hearts that break the AI mold
No need for external messages anymore
For you are in unison through your hearts.

jem®

The Chessboard

Let the light shine through
Let it shine over the dark
Let the world show its miseries
For you to awaken from the dark.

Everything is chaos
It has always been
You did not see it
For you were asleep in the dark.

Everything was hidden from you
In plain sight, you were playing along
The pieces having been moved around
For you to react and fight against the "enemy".

The chess pieces have been you and me
The players outside the board
Playing you to move around
For you to win or lose your life.

Everything is now shown
The players continue playing
But you do not move anymore
For you are now outside the gameboard.

You have become your player
You have discovered your potential
You have become limitless
For you are connecting to who you are.

jeannette meier Ph.D.

The world is showing you the play
Chaos, problem, and solution
No need for anyone to "save" you
For you are the light of your life.

The fights and separation are over
United, you stand in love and peace
In awareness of what there is
For you have awakened to the Truth.

Let your light shine through
Let you stay united in love and peace
Let the players disappear
For you and me are powerful in Oneness.

Together we are limitless!

jem®

Game Of Minds

What is an activist?
Is it someone speaking up for what there is?
There is always a label for everything
Why not be who you are?

Society labels everything
What does it matter "what" you are?
When being in love with who you are
For you are love and nothing else.

Labelling is separation
It is boxing you into a concept
Why the differentiation?
For you are who you are.

Does it make a difference to you
If you are label X or label Y?
For you to continue being the same
A perfectly imperfect being.

Separation is a game of minds
Separation is an illusion
For you are entangled with me
In the Oneness of who we are.

jem®

jeannette meier Ph.D.

You Are The Universe

You are pure love
You are limitless potential
A powerful being that has been hiding
Behind the curtains of illusion.

You are unconditional love
You are the Universe
A powerful being that does not know what it is
Other than what it is being told.

Let your light shine through
Let your power enlighten the world
You are free to be who you are
How should i tell you this?

Freedom to love
Freedom to live
Freedom to be
Freedom to co-create.

No one to stop your expansion
No one to put you down
Who knows more about you?
The infinite being that you are.

Live in freedom for who you are
Express the love that you are
Enlighten the world with your light
You are the Universe.

i love you.

jem®

Bibliography

Antic, Ivan. *Samadhi "Unity of Consciousness and Existence"*. Ivan Antic. 2018.

Cutler, Peter. *The Zen of Love*. 1st ed., N-Lightenment LLC, 2017.

Dr. Dispenza, Joe. *Becoming Supernatural "How Common People Are Doing the Uncommon"*. 1st ed., Hay House, Inc. 2017.

Erway, Daniel (aka. Nirmala). *Living from the Heart*. Endless Satsang Foundation, 2008.

Goddard, Neville. *The Complete Reader. Awakened Imagination & the Search*. First "AudioEnlightmentPress.Com" Printing, 2013.

Icke, David. *The Answer*. 1st ed., CPI Group Ltd. 2020.

Lent, Jeremy. *The Web of Meaning "Integrating Science and Traditional Wisdom to Find our Place in the Universe"*. Profile Books Ltd, 2021.

Ph.D McCraty, Rollin. Director of Research HeartMath Institute. *Science of the Heart "Exploring the Role of the Heart in Human Performance"*. Vol 2. HeartMath Institute. 2015.

OSHO. *The Chakra Book "Energy and Healing Power of the Subtle Body"*.

OSHO Media International. 2015.

Zukav, Gary. *The Seat of the Soul.* 25th ed., Simon and Schuster Paperbacks. 2014.

About The Author

jeannette meier Ph.D. guides you in uncovering your uniqueness and leadership power by listening to your heart and connecting to your freedom to be who you are and create what you love.

She graduated in 1996 in Systems Engineering and has worked in the IT business world since then. Jeannette has worked for multi-site, multi-cultural, and multi-language teams throughout Europe, the USA, and Latin

America since 1997, including business process consultancy at UNICEF.

In 2012, she founded the social enterprise YouTooday, which led to the Positive iMPACT Movement. This movement integrates the Leadership CiRCLE for the New Earth, which she passionately leads.

Jeannette is a Doctor of Philosophy specializing in Conscious-Centered Living. She has a bachelor's and a Master's degree in Metaphysical Science.

She is a socially conscious leader—a true leader—who applies her wisdom in everything she does. She explores, experiences, and practices living in freedom to be who she is and to create what she loves.

She co-creates with others to inspire and encourage everyone to be leaders for themselves.

Jeannette does not believe in governments or corporations; she believes in men and women and their limitless potential. Hence, she co-creates the New Earth by being the change she wants to see and sharing what she is: Love, Uniqueness, and Co-Creation.